SESAME STREET®

TOUGH TOPICS

Talking about
Deployment

A Sesame Street
Resource

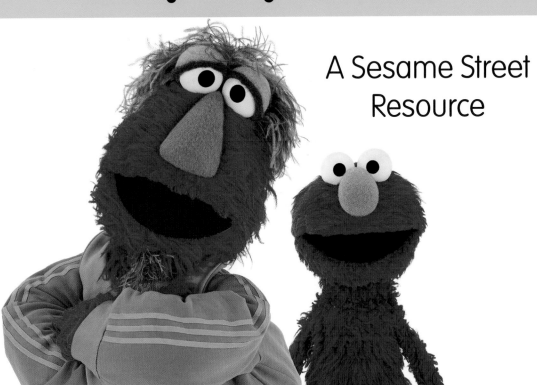

Charlotte Reed

Lerner Publications ◆ Minneapolis

Dear Grown-Up,

The more comfortable you are talking with children about the challenges they face, the more of a difference you can make in their lives. In this series, *Sesame Street* friends provide caregivers and educators a starting point to discuss, process, and offer support on tough topics. Together, we can help kids learn coping and resilience-building techniques to help them face tough challenges such as divorce, grief, and more.

Sincerely,
the Editors at Sesame Workshop

Table of Contents

What Is Deployment?

Sometimes people who work in the military are deployed. They have to go away for a while for their job.

When Elmo's daddy was deployed, Elmo did lots of things to get ready!

Dealing with Deployment

Before your loved one is deployed, you can spend time together. You might read together or play a game.

On the day your loved one leaves, you can give them a big hug and say goodbye. You might feel sad or upset. You might have a lot of questions too.

When your loved one is deployed, you can still do special things together.

You can both say good night to the moon every night.

Even though you're far away, you're both looking up at the same sky!

11

When your loved one is deployed, other grown-ups who love you will help take care of you. Maybe a neighbor will bring you to school, or you'll spend more time with your grandparents.

When Elmo's daddy is away, Elmo does more things with Elmo's mommy.

13

There are many ways to stay in touch with your loved one. You can call them on the phone.

When I'm apart from Abuela, I call her on the phone.

You can write them letters and emails. You can also draw them a picture!

Remember your loved one learned how to do their job. They work hard with their team to do the job well . . . together.

Everyone works together to stay safe!

17

Sometimes you might not know when a loved one is coming home. While they're gone, you can mark each day on the calendar.

Remember that they'll be home as soon as they can.

Make a list of all the things you want to do with them when they're back!

You and your loved one may be apart, but your love keeps your hearts close.

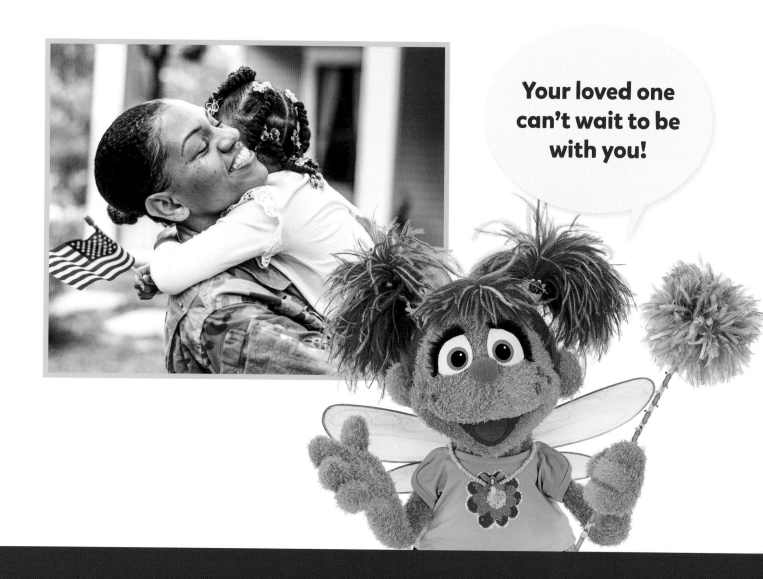

Your loved one can't wait to be with you!

What You Can Do

You can make a "hug me" pillow to snuggle with while your loved one is deployed.

1. With your loved one, choose one of their shirts. You can pick one that reminds you of them!

2. With the help of a grown-up, sew the neck and armholes of the shirt closed.

3. Fill the shirt with stuffing to create a pillow!

4. Now your grown-up can sew the shirt closed at the bottom.

5. Hug the pillow when you miss your loved one!

Glossary

calendar: something that shows days, weeks, and months of a year

deployed: when someone in the military is away for their job

job: what someone does for work

team: a group of people who work together

Read More

Chang, Kirsten. *Military Service*. Minneapolis: Bellwether Media, 2022.

Miller, Marie-Therese. *Parents Here and There: A Kid's Guide to Deployment*. Minneapolis: Lerner Publications, 2021.

Murray, Julie. *My Military Parent*. Minneapolis: Abdo Kids, 2021.

Explore more resources that help kids (and their grown-ups!) provided by Sesame Workshop, the nonprofit educational organization behind Sesame Street. Visit https://sesameworkshop.org/tough-topics/.

Photo Acknowledgments

Image credits: SDI Productions/Getty Images, pp. 4, 8; 2K Studio/Getty Images, p. 6; GizemBDR/Getty Images, p. 10; Westend61/Getty Images, p. 11; faidzzainal/Getty Images, 12 (top); evgenyatamanenko/Getty Images, p. 12 (middle); Jose Luis Pelaez Inc/Getty Images, pp. 12 (bottom), 13; EVAfotografie/Getty Images, p. 15; miodrag ignjatovic/Getty Images, p. 16; hsyncoban/Getty Images, p. 18; MoMo Productions/Getty Images, p. 20; Capuski/Getty Images, p. 21.

Cover: Jacob Lund/Shutterstock.

Index

For my father—one of the few and the proud

Lerner Publications Company
An imprint of Lerner Publishing Group, Inc.
241 First Avenue North
Minneapolis, MN 55401 USA

For reading levels and more information, look up this title at www.lernerbooks.com.

Main body text set in Mikado. Typeface provided by HVD.

Designer: Laura Otto Rinne **Photo Editor:** Nicole Berglund
Lerner team: Connie Kuhnz, Sue Marquis

Library of Congress Cataloging-in-Publication Data

Names: Reed, Charlotte, 1997- author.
Title: Talking about deployment : a Sesame Street resource / Charlotte Reed
Description: Minneapolis : Lerner Publications, 2024. | Series: Sesame Street tough topics | Includes bibliographical references and index. | Audience: Ages 4–8 | Audience: Grades K–1 | Summary: "Young readers learn with their friends from Sesame Street about deployment. They discover more about having a loved one deployed and how to live well and stay connected while their person is away"— Provided by publisher.
Identifiers: LCCN 2023038159 (print) | LCCN 2023038160 (ebook) | ISBN 9798765620205 (library binding) | ISBN 9798765629666 (paperback) | ISBN 9798765637326 (epub)
Subjects: LCSH: Children of military personnel—Juvenile literature. | Deployment (Strategy)—Psychological aspects—Juvenile literature. | Families of military personnel—Juvenile literature.
Classification: LCC UB403 .R443 2024 (print) | LCC UB403 (ebook) | DDC 355.1/2—dc23/eng/20231108

LC record available at https://lccn.loc.gov/2023038159
LC ebook record available at https://lccn.loc.gov/2023038160

Manufactured in the United States of America
1-1009964-51825-1/23/2024

24

Great Figures in Black H

W.E.B.
DU BOIS

Theia Lake

PowerKiDS
press

Published in 2024 by The Rosen Publishing Group, Inc.
2544 Clinton Street, Buffalo, NY 14224

Portions of this work were originally authored by Hilary Lochte and published as *W.E.B. Du Bois*. All new material in this edition was authored by Theia Lake.

Editor: Theresa Emminizer
Book Design: Rachel Rising

Photo Credits: Cover, W.E.B. (William Edward Burghardt) Du Bois, 1868-1963/Libary of Congress; Cover, pp. 1-32 Wall to wall/Shutterstock.com; Cover, pp. 1,3, 30-32 ReVelStockArt/Shutterstock.com; p. 4 https://commons.wikimedia.org/wiki/File:W.E.B._DuBois_Signature.svg; p. 5 View_Point/Shutterstock.com; p. 6 Albert Pego/Shutterstock.com; p. 7 Great Barrington High School, Class of 1884/New York Public Library; p. 9 KennStilger47/Shutterstock.com; p. 10 https://commons.wikimedia.org/wiki/File:Berlin_Universitaet_um_1850.jpg; p. 11 Marcio Jose Bastos Silva/Shutterstock.com; p. 13 https://commons.wikimedia.org/wiki/File:W.E.B._Du_Bois.jpg; p. 15 https://commons.wikimedia.org/wiki/File:W.E.B._Du_Bois_by_James_E._Purdy,_1907_(cropped).jpg; p. 17 Ammak/Shutterstock.com; p. 17 https://commons.wikimedia.org/wiki/File:The_Souls_of_Black_Folk_title_page.jpg; pp. 19, 27 Everett Collection/Shutterstock.com; p. 21 https://commons.wikimedia.org/wiki/File:Tuskegee_Institute_-_faculty.jpg; p. 22 https://commons.wikimedia.org/wiki/File:Niagara_Movement_delegates,_Boston,_Mass.,_1907.png; p. 23 https://commons.wikimedia.org/wiki/File:Niagara_movement_meeting_in_Fort_Erie,_Canada,_1905.jpg; p. 25 Joe Seer/Shutterstock.com; p. 26 https://commons.wikimedia.org/wiki/File:Professor_W._E._Burghardt_Du_Bois,_sociologist.png; p. 28 MM_photos/Shuttestock.com.

Names: Lake, Theia.
Title: W. E. B. Du Bois / Theia Lake.
Description: New York : Powerkids Press, 2024. | Series: Great figures in black history | Includes glossary and index.
Identifiers: ISBN 9781642826906 (pbk.) | ISBN 9781642826913 (library bound) | ISBN 9781642826920 (ebook)
Subjects: LCSH: Du Bois, W. E. B. (William Edward Burghardt), 1868-1963--Juvenile literature. | African Americans--Biography--Juvenile literature. | African American intellectuals--Biography--Juvenile literature. | African American civil rights workers--Biography--Juvenile literature.
Classification: LCC E185.97.D73 L354 2024 | DDC 323.092 B--dc23

Manufactured in the United States of America

CPSIA Compliance Information: Batch #CSPK24. For further information contact Rosen Publishing at 1-800-237-9932.

Find us on

CONTENTS

W. E. B. (William Edward Burghardt) Du Bois was an American intellectual, or thinker, writer, leader, and social **reformer**. He spent his life studying and working to change society for the better.

Du Bois's work was a key part of the advancement of Black rights during the early 1900s. Through his writing and speeches, Du Bois raised awareness about the kinds of struggles Black Americans faced. He spoke out against the systems that kept Black people in **poverty**. He advocated, or fought for, higher education for Black people, believing that well-educated leaders would lift the Black community out of **oppression**. By his death at age 95 in 1963, Du Bois had helped carve the path toward racial equality.

DU BOIS'S SIGNATURE

This sculpture shows W. E. B. Du Bois in the "thinker" pose.
Du Bois was a deep thinker and had a great thirst for knowledge.

GREAT BARRINGTON

Du Bois was born on February 23, 1868, in the small town of Great Barrington, Massachusetts. His mother, Mary Burghardt, and her family raised him. He had very little contact with his father, Alfred Du Bois.

W. E. B.'s family were some of the few Black people living in Great Barrington. Du Bois's classmates and playmates were all white. However, Du Bois said he didn't experience much **discrimination** during his childhood.

Du Bois had a happy childhood. He was a great student and graduated from Great Barrington High School in 1884. He was the school's first Black graduate.

GREAT BARRINGTON TODAY

Off to College

After high school, Du Bois began working as a reporter in Great Barrington. He would have liked to have gone to college, but he didn't have enough money to do so. However, a group of people from Great Barrington put together the money to further Du Bois's education. He went to Fisk University, a Black college in Nashville, Tennessee.

This photo shows the Great Barrington High School, Class of 1884. Du Bois is on the far left.

FISK UNIVERSITY

Du Bois came to Tennessee in 1885 at 17 years old. His years at Fisk University were his first time surrounded by almost all Black people. Du Bois and his classmates lived a protected life at the college, but off school grounds, life was different.

Du Bois taught in **rural** Tennessee during his summers. Many of his students came from sharecropping families. Sharecroppers raised crops for landowners. They were paid part of the money from the sales. This system kept many Black families in poverty.

Du Bois's students wanted to go to school but couldn't attend often enough because their families needed them to work. Du Bois worried that education wouldn't be enough to help these children.

The Post-Civil War South

Life for most Black people in Tennessee was much different from what Du Bois had experienced in his hometown in Massachusetts. During Reconstruction (the period after the end of the Civil War and slavery), most Black people in the United States faced discrimination and mistreatment. This was especially true in the South.

Fisk University in Nashville, Tennessee.

Du Bois had a deep love of learning. After he graduated from Fisk University in 1888, he decided to go back to Massachusetts. He had long dreamed of going to Harvard University. While at Harvard, Du Bois earned his bachelor's degree in **philosophy** in 1890. He also earned his master's degree in history in 1892.

FRIEDRICH WILHELM UNIVERSITY

Still, he wanted to learn more! Du Bois then went to Germany, where he studied at Friedrich Wilhelm University for two years before going back to Harvard. In 1895, he earned his doctorate degree (PhD) in history. He was the first Black student at Harvard to do so.

The W. E. B. Du Bois Medal is now the highest honor in the field of African and African American studies at Harvard. The school awarded the medal to writer

While Du Bois was earning his doctorate at Harvard, he was hired by Wilberforce University, a Black college in Ohio. Du Bois began working at Wilberforce in 1894, teaching Greek and Latin. Later, he taught German.

He then went on to work at the University of Pennsylvania. The school asked him to study the lives of Black people living in Philadelphia. As part of this work, Du Bois met and spoke with thousands of Black people living in the city. He published the findings of his study in 1899 in *The Philadelphia Negro: A Social Study*. Negro is an outdated word for Black. Du Bois hoped his report would help readers better understand the lives of Philadelphia's Black community.

The Progressive Era

The Progressive Era was a period of social reform during the late 1800s and early 1900s. During this time, social studies and reports were published to help the public better understand the problems facing different groups of people. *The Philadelphia Negro: A Social Study* was the first scholarly, or educational, race study of a city.

The Philadelphia Negro: A Social Study looked into the problems
facing the Black community in Philadelphia

Du Bois met Nina Gomer while he was teaching at Wilberforce University. The couple married on May 12, 1896.

In 1897, the Du Boises had a son named Burghardt Gomer Du Bois. Sadly, Burghardt grew ill with a disease, or sickness, called diphtheria. Burghardt died on May 24, 1899, when he was only 2 years old.

The loss was heartbreaking for W. E. B. and his wife. He said: "The child's death tore our lives in two." In October 1900, they had another child, a daughter named Nina "Yolande" Du Bois. Yolande helped the family heal, but they never forgot Burghardt. W. E. B. and Nina were married until she died in 1950.

Deadly Racism

During his son's illness, Du Bois had firsthand experience of the deadly truth of **racism** at work. The Du Boises had trouble finding a doctor to treat their young son. There were few Black doctors in Atlanta, where they were living at the time. Few white doctors would treat Black patients or help a Black child.

This portrait of Du Bois was taken in 1907

THE SOULS OF BLACK FOLK

In 1897, Du Bois went to teach at Atlanta University in Georgia. While there, he continued to research, or study, and write. He also gave speeches throughout the United States and overseas. Du Bois spoke out about the racism and poverty that Black Americans faced.

In 1903, he published a collection of essays, or articles, called *The Souls of Black Folk*. The book is one of the earliest **sociology** publications in American history. It's still widely read today!

In *The Souls of Black Folk*, Du Bois talked about how racism affected people's lives and how it could be fought. He wrote: "We have no right to sit silently by while the **inevitable** seeds are sown for a harvest of **disaster** to our children, Black and white."

An Important Publication

Though published more than a hundred years ago, *The Souls of Black Folk* has remained an important book and has been reprinted many times over. It offers readers an understanding of history, of Du Bois himself, and of the problems facing Black Americans and how Du Bois felt they should be fixed.

THE

SOULS OF BLACK FOLK

ESSAYS AND SKETCHES

BY

W. E. BURGHARDT DU BOIS

SECOND EDITION

CHICAGO
A. C. McCLURG & CO.
1903

This is the title page of *The Souls of Black Folk*. The book was very popular and was reprinted twice within two months of coming out.

WASHINGTON

Booker T. Washington was another great leader, thinker, and educator. Born into slavery, Washington went on to found Tuskegee Institute, a school in Alabama, in 1881.

Washington thought that industrial education (farming, carpentry, cooking, etc.) would help Black people by giving them practical skills and financial safety. Du Bois disagreed. Du Bois thought it was important to teach Black people to be leaders and thinkers. He wanted Black people to learn classical subjects (philosophy, history, etc.) as he had.

Du Bois believed in what he called "The Talented Tenth." His idea was that a small group of educated Black people, like himself, would lead the Black community out of poverty and oppression.

Two Approaches

Washington and Du Bois presented two different approaches, or ways of dealing with, the problem of racial oppression. Du Bois knew industrial training would help many Black people, and Washington knew a classical education was important to help create Black leaders. Both men cared deeply about helping the Black community but couldn't agree on approaches.

Both Du Bois and Washington were well known and respected. Du Bois worried that the focus on industrial education would take away support from schools that taught classical education, such as Atlanta University where he worked.

Du Bois feared that white people only supported Washington's ideas because that meant Black people would be kept in lower-level, lower-paid jobs. He felt Washington's ideas pushed Black people to accept **segregation** and oppression. Du Bois felt educating Black people as leaders was the best way to give them voices and make sure they had the power to change society for the better.

White Support

Washington had the support of many powerful white philanthropists, or people who give money for social causes. These men and women helped raise money for his school. Some Black leaders criticized, or spoke out against, Washington for not pushing hard enough to change the position of Black Americans in society. Many felt his ideas about hard work didn't face the full problem of discrimination.

BOOKER T. WASHINGTON   ANDREW CARNEGIE

Washington had many wealthy white supporters, such as Andrew Carnegie, pictured here with Washington on a visit to Tuskegee Institute in 1906.

A MEETING OF MINDS

In 1905, Du Bois brought together a group of 29 Black leaders to discuss, or talk about, ways to fight segregation. They met in Niagara Falls, Canada, and named their group The Niagara Movement. Together, the leaders wrote a "Declaration of Principles," in which they identified what rights they felt were most important to better the lives of Black Americans. They wanted freedom of speech, the right to equal education, and an end to segregation laws.

The Niagara Movement grew to more than 150 members in 17 states. However, it couldn't gain the amount of support and money it needed. The white public preferred Washington's message to Du Bois's. The Niagara Movement ended in 1909.

The Niagara Movement laid the groundwork for the National Association for the Advancement of Colored People.

FROM TEACHER TO ACTIVIST

The National Association for the Advancement of Colored People (NAACP) was formed in 1909. In it, It was an organization of white and Black **activists** who came together to fight for equal rights for Black Americans.

In 1910, Du Bois left Atlanta University to work for the NAACP in New York. He acted as a researcher for the group and became the first editor of its monthly journal *The Crisis*. Under Du Bois's leadership, *The Crisis* reported on discrimination and **violence** against Black people across the nation. In 1915, an article listed more than 2,700 **lynchings** that had taken place over the past 30 years. By 1920, *The Crisis* had over 100,000 readers.

The NAACP

The NAACP continues its social justice work today, more than 100 years later. *The Crisis* was a big reason for the growth of the NAACP and is still published today. Du Bois worked as the journal's editor until 1934. At that point he left the NAACP because he disagreed with the group's thoughts on segregation.

NAACP

fter some tim   4 to 1948.

After parting with the NAACP, Du Bois went back to teach at Atlanta University, where he stayed for another decade, or 10 years.

At the end of World War II (1939–1945), Du Bois became an activist for peace. He spoke out against war and especially the use of nuclear weapons. Du Bois's peaceful views didn't make him popular. But he continued to speak out about what he believed in anyway.

The U.S. government went as far as to claim that Du Bois was working with the Soviet Union (now Russia). Du Bois was arrested but not charged because there was no proof against him. Unfortunately, the harm was done. Du Bois was frowned upon by many after this event.

This photo shows the aftermath of the nuclear weapon that was dropped on Hiroshima, Japan, in 1945.

A LIFE OF WORK

Du Bois continued to work into his old age. He was invited to speak all over the world and at age 90 went on a speaking tour of Europe, the Soviet Union, and China.

In 1961, Du Bois moved to Ghana. He planned to make an encyclopedia (set of books about a certain subject) of Africa. Du Bois passed away in Ghana on August 27, 1963. He was 95 years old.

Du Bois's dream of racial equality wasn't realized within his lifetime. But his work and ideas were, and continue to be, an important part of civil rights history and understanding the harmful effects of racism.

TIMELINE OF W. E. B. DU BOIS

1868
William Edward Burghardt Du Bois is born February 23 in Great Barrington, Massachusetts.

1884
Du Bois becomes the first Black person to graduate from Great Barrington High School.

1888
Du Bois graduates from Fisk University.

1894
Wilberforce University hires Du Bois as a professor.

1895
Du Bois earns a doctoral degree from Harvard.

1896
• Du Bois marries Nina Gomer.
• Burghardt Gomer Du Bois is born.

1897
• Du Bois accepts a teaching position at Atlanta University.
• Du Bois's research for the University of Pennsylvania is published.

1899
Burghardt Du Bois dies.

1900
Nina "Yolande" Du Bois is born.

1903
Du Bois publishes *The Souls of Black Folk*.

1905
Du Bois founds The Niagara Movement.

1910
Du Bois becomes the first editor of the NAACP's journal, *The Crisis*.

1934
Du Bois steps down from *The Crisis* and returns to Atlanta University.

1963
Du Bois dies in Ghana on August 27.

GLOSSARY

activist: Someone who acts strongly in support of or against an issue.

disaster: Something that causes much suffering and loss for many people.

discrimination: Unfair treatment based on factors such as a person's race, age, religion, or gender.

inevitable: Bound to happen.

lynching: Killing someone for a supposed offense without a legal trial.

oppression: Cruel and unfair treatment.

philosophy: The study of the basic ideas about knowledge, right and wrong, reasoning, and the value of things.

poverty: The state of being poor.

racism: The belief that one group or race of people is better than another group or race.

reformer: Someone who seeks to change society for the better.

rural: Having to do with the country.

segregation: The separation of people based on race, class, sex, gender, or ethnicity.

sociology: The study of people and society.

violence: The use of bodily force to hurt, harm, or destroy.

FOR MORE INFORMATION

Books

Bayne, Bijan C. *Black Trailblazers: 30 Courageous Visionaries Who Broke Boundaries, Made a Difference, and Paved the Way.* Kansas City, MO: Andrews McMeel Publishing, 2022.

Santella, Andrew. *The NAACP: An Organization Working to End Discrimination.* North Mankato, MN: The Child's World, 2021.

Websites

Hutchins Center for African and African American Research

hutchinscenter.fas.harvard.edu/web-dubois

Read about W. E. B.'s life, studies, and work.

NAACP

naacp.org/find-resources/history-explained/civil-rights-leaders/web-du-bois

Learn more about W. E. B. Du Bois, his legacy, and his work in the NAACP.

INDEX